LINKING
Math and
techNoLogy

grade 3

Creative Publications®

This book is based on the MathLand series, which was written by Linda Charles, Micaelia Randolph Brummett, Heather McDonald, and Joan Westley.

Writer: Lynn Sanchez
Project Editor: Nora Sweeny
Classroom Coordinator: Ema Arcellana

Creative Director: Ken Shue
Art Director: Janice Kawamoto
Cover Illustration: David Broad
Production Coordinator: Ed Lazar
Production Services: Morgan-Cain & Associates

©1995 Creative Publications
1300 Villa Street
Mountain View, CA 94041

Printed in the United States of America.
ISBN: 1-56107-830-1
1 2 3 4 5 6 7 8 9 10 99 98 97 96 95

CONTENTS

Your guide to Linking Math and technology

- **You can create a mathematical and technology-rich environment for students.**

  In this environment students are encouraged to think, invent, investigate, and make connections using the computer. As a guide and facilitator, you can ask questions or propose challenges, and then stand back, observe, and listen.

- **The investigations in this book invite a diversity of approaches.**

  Different ways of thinking are expected and encouraged. Every child will bring something different and unique to the experience and gain something different from the experience.

- **Students use blank paper for these investigations.**

  Students can approach the tasks at their own level and think about it in their own way—there's room for different levels of prior knowledge, different languages, and all kinds of thinking. Authentic work produced by students who tested the program is featured throughout the book.

- **Manipulative materials are essential for mathematical understanding.**

  Students use manipulative models to enhance their understandings of mathematical concepts. The kit provided with this book has appropriate materials for the investigations.

- **Computers help students see mathematical ideas in a new light.**

  By using computers, students can develop new strategies for solving mathematical problems. They may notice that the computer provides a more accurate way of making a graph, or that the changing data that is reflected quickly on the screen graph shows how the pattern holds, or that convincing someone of their ideas may be easier when the elements of animation and sound and color are added.

- **Computers become new tools for clarifying and deepening understandings of mathematical ideas.**

  The computer is much more than just an electronic paper and pencil. As the students develop the skills necessary to become proficient with these new tools, the results can be astounding—what the students create using these programs are highly sophisticated projects. But the students also learn that what the computer produces is the direct result of their creativity, thoughtfulness, and understanding of the mathematical concepts.

The thoughtful and creative use of technology can greatly improve both the quality of the curriculum and the quality of children's learning. Integrating calculators and computers into school mathematics programs is critical in meeting the goals of a redefined curriculum.

National Council of Teachers of Mathematics
Curriculum and Evaluation Standards for School Mathematics

How is Linking Math and Technology organized?

This book is organized into ten investigations. These in-depth investigations are designed to let you know what to do each step of the way.

These NCTM strands are integrated throughout the investigations:

- **Number relations**
- **Logic and language**
- **Probability and statistics**
- **Patterns and functions**
- **Data analysis**

- **Measurement**
- **Discrete mathematics**
- **Geometry and visual thinking**
- **Algebra**

In these investigations, students are doing real math all the time.

- **They produce original reports and projects.**
- **They organize their material in ways that make sense to them.**
- **Their solutions reflect their personal understandings.**
- **They use manipulatives to make learning real.**
- **Their work together promotes cooperation and results in richer thinking.**

How can i integrate these investigations in my curriculum?

Use these investigations to connect math and computers in the classroom as supplements or extensions to your regular mathematics curriculum. The investigations can enhance other curriculum areas as well—social studies, art, language arts, science, and so on. These ten investigations correlate with units in the MathLand series (see the chart on page 1), but they may be used in any order you choose to augment your curriculum. Once the students have worked through the tutorials and are familiar with the software, they are knowledgeable enough to do the investigations in any order you specify.

What materials will i need to do the investigations?

The Classroom Manipulatives Kit provides materials for the whole class and is used for the curriculum-based initiating activity. It includes:

- **Pattern Blocks**
- **Coins**
- **Rainbow Tiles**
- **Numeral Dice**
- **Rainbow Cubes**

Other materials you will need:

- **blank paper (full, half, and quarter sheets)**
- **pencils, crayons, markers**
- **paste or glue sticks**
- **tape**
- **stapler**
- **calculators**

How are these investigations organized?

Each four-page investigation is made up of the components listed below. These components are designed so that you can cover each investigation easily, using numbered guidelines and step-by-step computer procedures.

WHAT IS THIS INVESTIGATION ABOUT?

You'll find a brief overview and unifying mathematical ideas covered in the investigation.

PLANNING FOR THE INVESTIGATION

You'll see a list of the materials needed for the investigation—manipulatives, paper, supplies, and preparation—as well as what software you'll use.

BEFORE THE INVESTIGATION

You'll complete a brief whole-class activity that triggers student thinking before you begin the investigation.

INITIATING THE INVESTIGATION

These numbered guidelines provide you with a step-by-step process to follow, with clear instructions for both you and your students. Words in bold italic are "teacher talk," and helpful hints for you are boxed in the margin. Diagrams and sample student work show what the students will be doing at various stages in the investigation.

INTEGRATING SOFTWARE INTO THE INVESTIGATION

These numbered instructions suggest how you might work with the students through the computer extension, with step-by-step computer procedures and shortcuts listed in the left margin. Sample student work provides a preview of what you can expect from your own students.

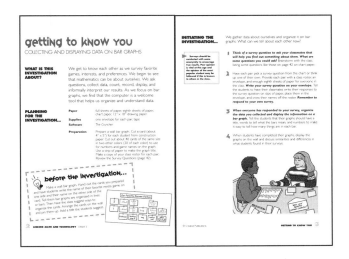

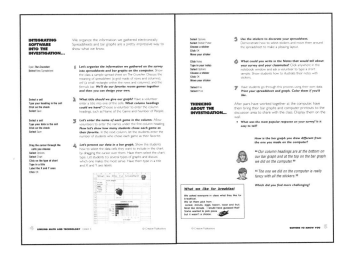

THINKING ABOUT THE INVESTIGATION

Here is your chance to learn from the students themselves what knowledge they have created from their work. There are sample assessment questions, and the dialog box shows how real students responded to the investigation.

How Should I Organize My Class For These Investigations?

The majority of these investigations are designed for pairs or groups of four students, with each child assigned a task—observer, director, operator, and checker; or writer, illustrator, sound recorder, and editor. Students should rotate roles each time they use the computer. Encourage students to teach one another what they have learned from previous computer experience or the tutorials. Teacher assistants, parent volunteers, and upper-grade students can also be trained to become computer experts. Give the class guidelines for using the computers: when they may use them, how to name their files, and when they can print or play back their work.

How Long Do These Investigations Take?

In a classroom with several computers, it may be possible for the class to complete each investigation over a few days. In a classroom where only one computer is available, you may want to complete **Initiating the Investigation** with the entire class, and then let groups of students complete the computer extension as time allows (over a period of days or weeks). Whether your class has one computer or many, **Thinking About the Investigation** is a good time to gather students together after they have all completed the investigation, to view each other's projects and to assess what was learned from the process.

What Software Have You Developed for My Classroom?

The two software tools for the intermediate grades are **The Cruncher** and **The Multimedia Workshop.** Both packages are available for the Macintosh or Windows, in English or Spanish, for single or multiple users.

The Cruncher, by Davidson and Associates, Inc., gives students in the intermediate grades the power to create projects that compute, graph, and teach math concepts in an exciting way. From their data, students can visualize and analyze their results with pie and scatter charts and bar and line graphs. Tutorials show each step of the formulas they use, and a powerful text-to-speech feature allows students to listen to words or numbers in their documents. The notebook and a library of colorful stickers, illustrations, and animation adds to the discourse of their work. *The Cruncher* includes three modules: the **Spreadsheet, Tutorials**, and **Projects**. The **Spreadsheet** has all the features students would expect to find in a professional spreadsheet program: mathematical operators, functions, and graphing. The **Tutorials** introduce the elements of spreadsheets and special features of *The Cruncher* in step-by-step, self-guided sequences. The **Projects** provide investigative situations with illustrated text and preformatted spreadsheets to give students more hands-on experience with the mathematical concepts.

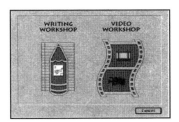

The Multimedia Workshop, by Davidson and Associates, Inc., allows students to plan, develop, and create documents and multimedia presentations. *The Multimedia Workshop* includes immense libraries of photographs, illustrations, sounds, and video clips on CD-ROM. Three modules that make up this sophisticated program are the **Writing Workshop**, **Paint Workshop**, and **Video Workshop**. The **Writing Workshop** is an elaborate word processing program that includes a spell-checker, thesaurus, and document templates. The **Paint Workshop** is a full-featured paint program. In it, photographs and clip art can be modified and backgrounds can be created with the many tools in the toolbox. The original art work created in the **Paint Workshop** can be printed directly or used in the students' published documents and video presentations. Students can use their art and text to create sophisticated multimedia presentations in the **Video Workshop.**

How can i get a running start with the software?

You can become familiar with the software by reading the user manuals, but spending actual "hands-on" time with the software is the fastest way. The tutorials provide a 30-minute overview of all the features you'll need for the investigations. The manuals also provide some useful tips on how to set up the software to make it easier for the students to use. Here are some suggestions:

- **Make computer folders or directories to hold the documents and files that the students create.**
- **Set preferences and defaults for the font, type size, sound, and so on that are appropriate for your students.**
- **Arrange and simplify the windows on the screen.**
- **Disable functions that are unnecessary.**

How should i introduce the software to the students?

It is important to set aside some time, especially in the beginning, so the students can freely explore the software. Give them a tour of the tutorials and templates. Before each investigation, review the menus, buttons, actions (especially **SAVE**), and folder locations so students can find their work when they need to! You may find it helpful to review software-specific terminology—*icons, files,* and *save,* for example—and demonstrate pertinent features, too.

is the software easy to use?

The ten investigations here have been specially designed for use with these two software packages. And the software has been tested and used by thousands of children. If you have problems with the software, you may find the online help menus and troubleshooting tips in the manuals helpful. If you have problems that can't be solved by referring to the manuals or using the online help menus, call the toll-free customer support numbers listed in the manuals.

PERFORMANCE TIPS FOR *THE CRUNCHER*

- Remember that all formulas must begin with an equal sign.
- ***The Cruncher*** calculates so quickly that students may miss the operation. When you demonstrate formulas or functions, click between the data and **Show** several times so they can see what is happening to the data within the cell.
- To create a chart, you must choose columns that are adjacent to one another.

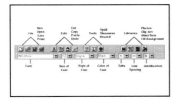

PERFORMANCE TIPS FOR *THE MULTIMEDIA WORKSHOP*

- ***The Multimedia Workshop*** produces several types of documents. Review with students how to recognize documents from the **Libraries**, **Writing Workshop**, **Scene Maker**, and **Sequencer**, and set up a system for project folders.
- To prevent crashes and error messages, set the memory to the size recommended by the developer.

Let's peek into our Linking Math and technology classroom.

DURING THE MATH INVESTIGATION

Students daydream about the home they would love to own; then they set out to design it! They use Rainbow Tiles to visualize and approximate areas. Then they make the floor plans on grid paper.

The students' first task is to design their dream homes using Rainbow Tiles. They find out that being limited to 50 tiles is a reality check—there just isn't enough space for all the rooms they'd like!

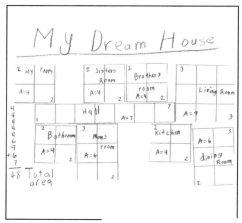

When they complete their design with Rainbow Tiles, students have to figure out a way to translate this information onto grid paper. Plotting their dream homes on paper makes them feel like first-class architects.

these students are linking the cruncher with their dream houses.

DURING THE TECHNOLOGY EXTENSION

Students enter their dream home data on *The Cruncher* and use the spreadsheet to calculate areas of the rooms and chart the results. *The Cruncher* makes it easy to use functions, formulas, or simple operations to come up with an impressive result.

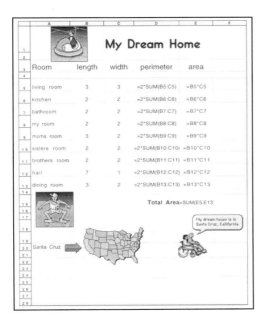

Planning where to put all the information is a challenge: what cells? what fonts? Should the data go in a column or a row? The students use the notebook to explain their thinking; that's helpful in assessment. During their exploration, students found that some of the stickers are animated—what a fun surprise!

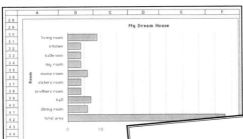

Students viewed the information in various graphs. They decide that the bar graph conveys the most information and print it to add to their portfolio.

Letter from a Teacher

This investigation required the students to plan and think ahead—that is something they haven't experienced much yet, so it was a challenge. It helped that the investigation built up to the computer work with the manipulatives and paper-and-pencil work. Some students used formulas to figure the area, others added. The students who used the formulas loved how quickly the computer could do the calculations! Many students asked me to add all of the pieces of this investigation to their portfolios.

Let's peek into our Linking Math and technology classroom.

DURING THE MATH INVESTIGATION

Students are challenged to design an animal park and make a map of it. They think about how to draw a scale model, and how to allocate space for both animals and people in their park.

For their first task, the students make a map of their park using Rainbow Tiles. This is not as easy as it looks—they must consider space limitations and the requirements set forth in their instructions. Oh no! Not all the animals the students want to include will fit in!

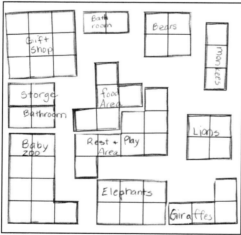

After they are satisfied with the tile plan, students transfer their plan onto grid paper. It's all beginning to make sense.

these students are linking the multimedia workshop with their animal parks.

DURING THE TECHNOLOGY EXTENSION

Students use their new knowledge to create video scenes about their animal park design. They assemble their scenes into a high-energy multimedia presentation using *The Multimedia Workshop*.

Students who enjoy art create some scenes in the **Paint Workshop**. Other students enjoy previewing and then adding clip art, photographs, and **QuickTime** movies from the **Libraries** to their scenes.

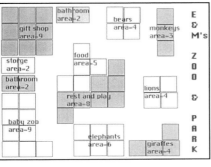

A student narrator explains the layout of the park, and how the area measurements were figured. She saves the sound file to use later in the movie. After all the groups have finished, the class plans an Animal Park Film Festival. The students are so proud of their work that they copy their presentations onto videotape to share with family members at home.

Letter from a Teacher

There was so much to do in this investigation, it appealed to the varied learning styles of my students. Some students researched to find what environments were best for the animals they wanted to include—others enjoyed figuring out how to best use the "90 tiles" of space! Some students didn't work on the computer as much as they would have liked—next time we'll have a clearer idea of how to divide the tasks up. Our presentations were so impressive the principal wrote about the project in her newsletter to parents.

Hardware requirements

To run **THE CRUNCHER,** you will need

For the Macintosh environment:
- Mac Classic or above
- 4 MB or more with 2 MB free RAM
- 13 MB on hard disk
- System 7.0 or higher
- Printer (highly recommended)

For the PC environment:
- IBM Compatible
- 80386 16 MHz or better
- 4 MB RAM
- 12 MB on hard disk
- Windows 3.1 or higher
- Sound card (recommended)
- Printer (highly recommended)

To run **THE MULTIMEDIA WORKSHOP,** you will need

For the Macintosh environment:
- LC or above
- 4 MB or more RAM for 256 colors; 8 MB or more for Thousands of Colors
- 8 MB on hard disk
- System 7.0 or higher
- CD-ROM Drive (highly recommended)
- Printer (highly recommended)
- Microphone (highly recommended)

For the PC environment:
- IBM Compatible
- 80486 25 MHz or better
- 4 MB minimum RAM (8 MB recommended)
- 20 MB on hard disk
- CD-ROM Drive (highly recommended)
- Windows 3.1 or higher
- Sound card (required)
- Printer (highly recommended)
- Microphone (highly recommended)

key Mathematical ideas covered

The ten investigations in this book correlate with the key mathematical ideas and projects in the MathLand series listed below:

Investigation	MathLand Project	Key Mathematical Ideas
Getting to Know You	**Unit 1/Week 1**	Data Analysis Number Relations
Thinking in "Bunches"	**Unit 2/Week 2**	Patterns Visual Thinking Logical Thinking Discrete Math
What's a Word Worth?	**Unit 3/Week 5**	Number Relations Logical Thinking Algebra
Rectangles Problems	**Unit 4/Week 2**	Number Relations Geometry
To Be...AND, OR, NOT ...To Be	**Unit 5/Week 2**	Logic Algebra Discrete Math
Thousands Collections	**Unit 6/Week 1**	Number Relations Discrete Math
Design a Dream House	**Unit 7/Week 2**	Measurement Visual Thinking Number Relations
Quilt Squares	**Unit 8/Week 2**	Geometry Visual Thinking Logical Thinking Number Relations
Animal Park	**Unit 9/Week 5**	Number Relations Measurement Visual Thinking Logical Thinking
Tally Ho!	**Unit 10/Week 1**	Probability Number Relations Discrete Math

getting to know you
COLLECTING AND DISPLAYING DATA ON BAR GRAPHS

WHAT IS THIS INVESTIGATION ABOUT?

We get to know each other as we survey favorite games, interests, and preferences. We begin to see that mathematics can be about *ourselves*. We ask questions, collect data, count, record, display, and informally interpret our results. As we focus on bar graphs, we find that the computer is a welcome tool that helps us organize and understand data.

PLANNING FOR THE INVESTIGATION...

Paper	full sheets of paper; eighth sheets of paper; chart paper; 12" × 18" drawing paper
Supplies	one envelope for each pair; tape
Software	*The Cruncher*
Preparation	Prepare a wall bar graph. Cut a card (about 4" × 5") for each student from construction paper. Cut out about 40 cards of the same size in two other colors (20 of each color) to use for numbers and game names on the graph. Use a strip of paper to make the graph title. Make a copy of your class roster for each pair. Review the Survey Questions (page 42).

before the investigation...

Make a wall bar graph. Hand out the cards you prepared and have students write the name of their favorite recess game on one side and their name on the other side of the card. Tell them bar graphs are organized in lines or bars. Then have the class suggest ways to organize the cards. Arrange the cards on the wall and pin them up. Add a title the students suggest.

INITIATING THE INVESTIGATION...

We gather data about ourselves and organize it on bar graphs. What can we tell about each other now?

> Surveys should be conducted with some anonymity to encourage true results. Peer opinion is vital at this age and the opinion of the most popular student may be followed if this is known to others in the class.

1 ***Think of a survey question to ask your classmates that will help you find out something about them. What are some questions you could ask?*** Brainstorm with the class, listing some questions like those on page 42 on chart paper.

2 Have each pair pick a survey question from the chart or think up one of their own. Provide each pair with a class roster, an envelope, and enough eighth sheets of paper for everyone in the class. **Write your survey question on your envelope.** Tell the students to have their classmates write their responses to the survey question on slips of paper, place them in the envelope, and cross their names off the roster. **Remember to respond to your own survey.**

3 ***When everyone has responded to your survey, organize the data you collected and display the information on a bar graph.*** Tell the students that their graphs should have a title, words to tell what the bars mean, and numbers to make it easy to tell how many things are in each bar.

4 When students have completed their graphs, display the graphs on the wall and discuss similarities and differences in what students found in their surveys.

INTEGRATING SOFTWARE INTO THE INVESTIGATION...

We organize the information we gathered electronically. Spreadsheets and bar graphs are a pretty impressive way to show what we know.

Open *The Cruncher*
Select New Spreadsheet

1 *Let's organize the information we gathered on the survey into spreadsheets and bar graphs on the computer.* Show the class a sample spread sheet on *The Cruncher.* Discuss the meaning of *spreadsheet* (a grid made of rows and columns), *cell* (a small rectangle within the rows and columns), and the *formula* bar. *We'll do our favorite recess games together and then you can design your own.*

Select a cell
Type your heading in the cell
Click on the check
Select Save

2 *What title should we give our graph?* Have a volunteer enter a title into one of the cells. *What column headings could we have?* Choose a volunteer to enter the column headings, such as Name of the Game and Number of People.

Select a cell
Type your data in the cell
Click on the check
Select Save

3 *Let's enter the name of each game in the column.* Allow volunteers to enter the names under the first column heading. *Now let's show how many students chose each game as their favorite.* In the next column, let the students enter the number of students who chose each game as their favorite.

Drag the cursor through the cells you choose
Select Options
Select Chart
Click on the type of chart
Type in a title
Label the X and Y axes
Click OK

4 *Let's present our data in a bar graph.* Show the students how to select the data cells they want to include in the chart by dragging the cursor over them. Have them select the chart type. Let students try several types of graphs and discuss which one makes the most sense. Have them type in a title and X and Y axis labels.

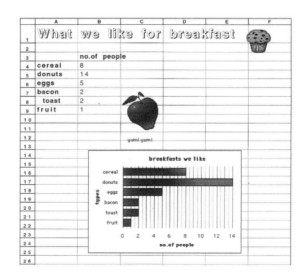

Select Options
Select Sticker Picker
Choose a sticker
Click OK
Move your sticker

Click Notes
Type in your notes
Select Options
Choose a sticker
Click OK
Move your sticker

Select File
Select Print

THINKING ABOUT THE INVESTIGATION...

5 *Use the stickers to decorate your spreadsheet.* Demonstrate how to select stickers and move them around the spreadsheet to make a pleasing layout.

6 *What could you write in the Notes that would tell about your survey and your classmates?* Click anywhere in the notebook window and ask a volunteer to type a short sample. Show students how to illustrate their notes with stickers.

7 Have students go through this process using their own data. *Print your spreadsheet and graph. Color them if you'd like.*

After pairs have worked together at the computer, have them bring their bar graphs and computer printouts to the discussion area to share with the class. Display them on the wall.

- *What was the most popular response on your survey? Is it easy to tell?*

How is the bar graph you drew different from the one you made on the computer?

" Our column headings are at the bottom on our bar graph and at the top on the bar graph we did on the computer."

" The one we did on the computer is really fancy with all the stickers."

Which did you find more challenging?

What we like for breakfast

We asked everyone in class what they like for breakfast.
We let them pick from :
cereal, donuts, eggs, bacon, toast and fruit.
Most like donuts. I would have guessed that!
Some wanted to pick pizza
but it wasn't a choice.

---

thinking in "bunches"

USING SKIP COUNTING TO SOLVE A REAL-WORLD PROBLEM

WHAT IS THIS INVESTIGATION ABOUT?

We use our skip-counting thinking to look for patterns as we solve a real-world problem. We're toy designers who make pinwheels out of Pattern Blocks. How many of each kind of block do we need? After we solve that problem, our creativity and marketing skills abound—we make a video presentation to convince the principal to purchase our Pattern Blocks pinwheels!

PLANNING FOR THE INVESTIGATION...

Manipulatives Kit	*For each pair:* one set of Pattern Blocks
Paper	full sheets of paper
Software	*The Multimedia Workshop*

before the investigation...

Today, you're going to be toy designers. Let's try to design some pinwheel toys. Take out the Pattern Blocks and show the students several pinwheel designs. Draw the designs, one design at a time, on the chalkboard. Introduce the idea of skip counting by asking the students, **How many Pattern Blocks would it take to make two of these** (pointing to one design)? **Three? How could we count the number of blocks faster? What can you tell us about skip counting? Did you count by threes? sixes? What patterns did you find?**

We design our own pinwheels and write order forms for the parts we need. All this thinking sets our minds spinning!

1. **Now it's your turn to make up a pinwheel toy.** Let the students work in pairs with Pattern Blocks to make a design and draw it on a sheet of paper.

2. **How many of each kind of block will it take to make one pinwheel for every student in the class?** Tell the students they should write up an order form listing the blocks needed for each student in the class to have a pinwheel. If time permits, the students can make more than one design and order form.

> Expect not only a wide variety of designs, but many different ways of organizing an order form. Some may seem more "organized" to an adult than others. Take the time to ask students to tell you about their thinking to better understand some of the ones you thought were "unorganized".

3. When the students have completed their designs and order forms, have them share these with the rest of the class, telling how they figured out the orders. **What blocks did you use in your pinwheel design? How many rhombuses did it take? triangles? How did you and your partner figure out your order?**

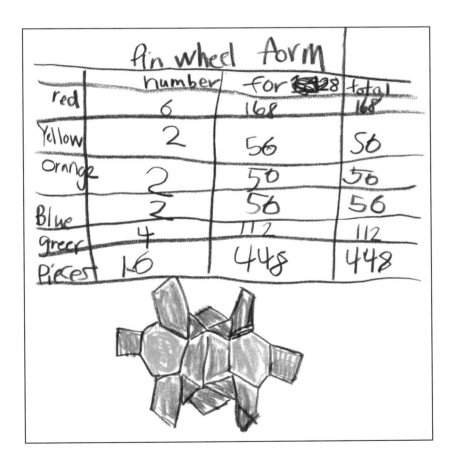

Pin wheel form

	number	for 28	total
red	6	168	168
Yellow	2	56	56
Orange	2	50	50
Blue	2	56	56
green	4	112	112
Pieces	16	448	448

INTEGRATING SOFTWARE INTO THE INVESTIGATION...

We make a video presentation to convince the principal to make a major pinwheel purchase. With our electronic tools, it's a breeze!

1 *Using your designs and order forms, I'd like you to make a video presentation on the computer to convince the principal to buy enough pinwheels for each student in our class.*

Open *The Multimedia Workshop*
Select New
Select Paint Workshop
Create your illustration
Save **your illustration**

2 *Let's start by making a drawing of one of our designs.* Have volunteers demonstrate different tools that could be useful—paint tools, shape tools, polygon tools, and so on. *Try exploring some of these tools as you make your pinwheels.*

Select Video Workshop Scene Maker
Import **your illustration**
Select a background
Type in your text
Save **your scene**

3 *Now we can put our drawing into a scene.* Discuss the Video Workshop Scene Maker toolbar. *We can make our scene really spiffy with a border or a background!* Demonstrate some of the background options. Let a few students demonstrate how to add text and choose different fonts, colors, styles, and sizes.

Click the microphone icon
Select Record
Record your narration
Save **your narration**

4 *What kind of sound would go with our scene? What could we say about it?* Pick a volunteer to narrate the scene.

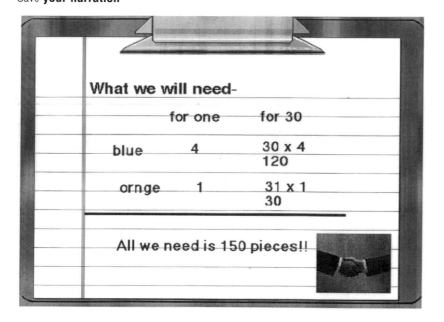

What we will need–

	for one	for 30
blue	4	30 x 4
		120
ornge	1	31 x 1
		30

All we need is 150 pieces!!

Our Pinwheel Design

Select Video Workshop Sequencer
Click on the first box on the
  video track
Import **your scene**
Select a transition
Place your transition
Save **your movie**

Click on the soundtrack
Open Libraries
Open Sound
Select some sound or music
Select your narration
Save **your movie**

Open Playback
Click Save & Play
Select Auto Play

THINKING ABOUT THE INVESTIGATION...

5 *After you have made several scenes, put them together to make a video presentation.* Let volunteers click on the various transitions to see how they work. Explain that transitions allow for a smooth break between scenes. Have students place several scenes and transitions.

6 *Let's add sound and music to the presentation.* Show students how to import their narration files or import files from the Sound or Music folder.

7 *Now let's watch our creation! Voila!* Play the movie the class has made.

I'd like you and your partner to make your own presentation on the computer. Include your design, order form, and anything else to help sell your pinwheel. Have the students go through the steps outlined here, and encourage them to explore the software.

Toward the end of the investigation, have pairs give their video presentations to the principal.

- *If you were writing an order for 100 pinwheels, how would you figure it out?*

What pinwheel would you design next time? Why?

" *I would make one with less Pattern Blocks. Then my order form would have been easier to figure out.* "

" *Me too. I would make a simpler pinwheel because it would be easier to draw on the computer.* "

Would anyone else make other changes?

What's a Word Worth?

USING NUMBER STRATEGIES TO SOLVE PROBLEMS

WHAT IS THIS INVESTIGATION ABOUT?

We use all kinds of strategies to add lots of numbers together. Paper and pencils, coins, calculators, and computers are all tools that help us solve this investigation's challenges. Displaying our work involves class cooperation to make and carry out a plan—this is important to learn, too.

PLANNING FOR THE INVESTIGATION...

Manipulatives Kit	*For each pair:* Coins (25 pennies, 12 nickels, 10 dimes, 4 quarters, and 2 half-dollars)
Paper	full sheets of paper, eighth sheets of paper, chart paper
Supplies	calculators
Software	*The Cruncher*
Preparation	Make a space on the wall for a class chart and display the heading What's A Word Worth? Make column headings as needed.

before the investigation...

Let's pretend each letter of the alphabet costs money. Let's say A is worth 1¢, B is worth 2¢, C is worth 3¢, and so on. Each letter costs one cent more than the last letter. Have students work with their partner to make an alphabet recording sheet that shows the value of each letter in the alphabet. After they have finished, ask, **How much is the letter M worth? the letter T?** Have a volunteer choose a word and add up what the word is worth with the class.

A = 1¢   I = 9¢
B = 2¢   J = 10¢   S = 19¢
C = 3¢   K = 11¢   T = 20¢
D = 4¢   L = 12¢   U = 21¢
E = 5¢   M = 13¢   V = 22¢
F = 6¢   N = 14¢   W = 23¢
G = 7¢   O = 15¢   X = 24¢
H = 8¢   P = 16¢   Y = 25¢
         Q = 17¢   Z = 26¢
         R = 18¢

seal 37¢

Mikiko 68¢

giraffe 52¢   pizza 78¢

INITIATING THE INVESTIGATION...

When we set a price on the letters of the alphabet, we discover how valuable words are!

1 **Use your code sheet to find the value of your first name.** Pairs work together to show the value of their first name using coins. They should make a recording that shows their first name, the coins needed to buy each letter, and the total value of their first name. **When you've finished this recording, put your first name and its value on a separate strip of paper.**

2 **Suppose we wanted to put our name strips in order? Whose name is the least expensive? most expensive?** Let the class choose a way to work together to order the names. On chart paper, write their plan and follow it to order the names on the wall chart.

3 **Now let's pick some other word categories to try.** Brainstorm with the class and list their suggestions on chart paper, such as animals, food, cities, and toys. Have the class vote to choose a word category. Start a new column on the wall chart with this category as the heading.

4 Let pairs produce as many strips as they can for each category. Each strip should include a word from the category and the value of that word. **Use different ways to find the total value of your word—coins, calculators, or paper and pencil. Remember to use your alphabet recordings to help you.**

5 As students finish a category, collect the strips and discuss with the class ways to arrange them on the wall chart. **Can anyone think of a plan that would work better than the way we ordered for first names?** After the strips are on the wall in order, discuss them with the class.

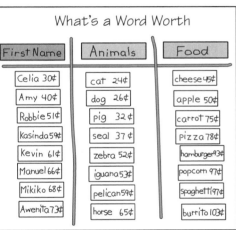

What's a Word Worth

First Name	Animals	Food
Celia 30¢	cat 24¢	cheese 45¢
Amy 40¢	dog 26¢	apple 50¢
Robbie 51¢	pig 32¢	carrot 75¢
Kasinda 59¢	seal 37¢	pizza 78¢
Kevin 61¢	zebra 52¢	hamburger 93¢
Manuel 66¢	iguana 53¢	popcorn 97¢
Mikiko 68¢	pelican 59¢	spaghetti 97¢
Awenita 73¢	horse 65¢	burrito 103¢

INTEGRATING SOFTWARE INTO THE INVESTIGATION...

Using the computer to make a spreadsheet helps us figure out how much a whole page is worth in the wink of an eye!

1 ***Let's use a spreadsheet to compute the values of words.*** Review the elements in a spreadsheet: rows, columns, and cells. ***We'll do one together, then you and your partner can make your own spreadsheet.***

Open ***The Cruncher***
Select New Spreadsheet
Select a cell
Type your title in the cell
Select Save

2 ***What title could we give our spreadsheet?*** Have a volunteer enter a title the students suggest into one of the cells. ***What column headings could we have?*** Choose a volunteer to enter two column headings, such as *Letter* and *Value*. ***First let's enter all the letters of the alphabet and their values.*** Let volunteers enter the letters from A to Z under the first column heading and the values from 1 to 26 under the second column heading.

Select a cell
Type your data in the cell
Click on the check
Select Save

3 ***Let's figure out some words that are different from the ones on our wall chart.*** Let students type a word under the next column (cat), and the value of each letter with a plus sign in the next column (3+1+22). Then show the students how to use the computer to get the sum. (Go up to the formula bar and add an equal sign before the first letter value and click the check). Go back and forth between the addends and then the sum with several words until students are comfortable with this.

	A	B	C	D	E	F
1	A WORDS (OR PETS) WORTH					
2						
3	letter	value	Pet	total value		
4	a	1	dog	27		
5	b	2	cat	24		
6	c	3	parrott	108		
7	d	4	snake	50		
8	e	5	hamster	84		
9	f	6	gerbil	53		
10	g	7				
11	h	8				
12	i	9				
13	j	10				
14	k	11				
15	l	12				
16	m	13				
17	n	14				
18	o	15				
19	p	16				
20	q	17				
21	r	18				

A parrott is worth alot!!!

Click Notes
Type in your notes
Select Options
Select Sticker Picker
Choose a sticker
Click OK
Move your sticker

Select File
Select Print

THINKING ABOUT THE INVESTIGATION...

4 *What could you write in the notes to tell about your spreadsheet?* Show the students how to edit and format what they type. *You could even try adding stickers.* Demonstrate how to select a sticker and then move it around on the spreadsheet.

5 Have pairs work at the computer to make a spreadsheet like the one the class did together. *Let the computer compute the value of three or four words you choose. Print your spreadsheet and notes. Add color to them if you'd like.*

After the students have finished their spreadsheets, invite them to share them with the class.

- *Which values were easiest to find—those that cost a little or those that cost a lot?*
- *Do words with the same value have the same letters? Why or why not?*

Tell us how you think the computer "thinks."

" *For the word* bird, *the computer thinks 2 + 9 + 18 + 4.* "

" *It does it really fast. Faster than I can think. I'm not sure how.* "

What do the rest of you think? Does someone have to tell the computer how to "think"?

	A	B	C	D
1	A WORDS (OR PETS) WORTH			
2				
3	letter	value	Pet	total value
4	a	1	dog	=B8+B18+B10
5	b	2	cat	=B6+B4+B23
6	c	3	parrott	=B19+B4+B21+B21+B18+B23+B23
7	d	4	snake	=B22+B17+B4+B14+B8
8	e	5	hamster	=B11+B4+B16+B22+B23+B8+B21
9	f	6	gerbil	=B10+B8+B21+B5+B12+B15
10	g	7		

rectangles problems
MULTIPLICATION THROUGH REAL-WORLD PROBLEMS

WHAT IS THIS INVESTIGATION ABOUT?

We explore multiplication as we investigate rectangular arrays. We are challenged to convince someone else that our solution is valid using some sophisticated computer tools. All in all, both playful and practical insights into the nature of multiplication are revealed to us as we discover more about mathematics and technology.

PLANNING FOR THE INVESTIGATION...

Manipulatives Kit *For each pair:*
40 Rainbow Cubes in the same color

Paper full sheets of paper, 1-cm grid paper (page 48), chart paper

Software *The Multimedia Workshop*

Preparation Pairs should have Rainbow Cubes all the same color. Number strips of paper from 1 to 20 and put them in a bag.

before the investigation...

Work with your partner and use 8 Rainbow Cubes to build a rectangle that is completely filled. When the pairs are finished, ask them to tell about their rectangles. Ask them to tell you about the number of rows and the number in each row. On the chalkboard, write a description for each rectangle using the "rows of" language and the multiplication equation. Continue until the four possibilities have been discussed. **Choose a number between 1 and 20. Record each rectangle on grid paper and write an equation to tell about it.**

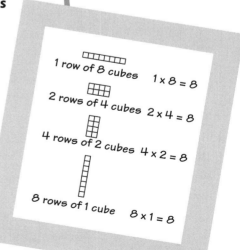

1 row of 8 cubes $1 \times 8 = 8$

2 rows of 4 cubes $2 \times 4 = 8$

4 rows of 2 cubes $4 \times 2 = 8$

8 rows of 1 cube $8 \times 1 = 8$

INITIATING THE INVESTIGATION...

We help the owner of a bicycle shop who needs our mathematical expertise to solve a tricky problem.

▶ It is important for third-graders to develop the ability to listen to a problem presented orally and write down the important details for themselves. If language difficulties make this too much of a challenge for some of your students, ask a volunteer to summarize the information on the chalkboard.

▶ A problem such as this has many different entry points. Some students will use objects to model the problem, others will sketch on scratch paper. The variety and diversity the students bring to this problem will provide lively discussions.

1 Present this real-world problem to the class and let them work together in pairs to solve it. Tell the problem twice, giving the students a chance to take notes. **The owner of a bicycle shop has a big problem. A shipment of bicycles, tricycles, and wagons just arrived, but none of them have wheels! The shipment had 5 bicycles, 7 tricycles, and 3 wagons. How many wheels do you think are needed?**

2 **Work with your partner and write your advice about how to solve this problem.** Write the problem information on chart paper as shown below so the students can refer to it.

3 As pairs work, circulate among them to learn about how they are thinking. If there is disagreement about how to solve the problem, let the final decision come through student debate rather than your instruction.

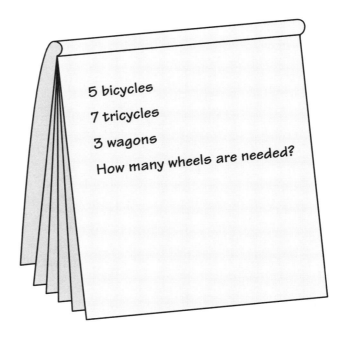

5 bicycles

7 tricycles

3 wagons

How many wheels are needed?

INTEGRATING SOFTWARE INTO THE INVESTIGATION...

The owner of the bicycle shop is really impressed with the presentations we make on the computer!

1 *Using your notes, I'd like you to make a presentation to convince the owner of the shop that you have solved his problem.*

Open *The Multimedia Workshop*
Select Paint Workshop
Select New
Create your illustration
Save **your illustration**

2 *You may want to begin your presentation with a drawing.* Show students how to access the Paint Workshop and have volunteers demonstrate different tools that could apply to this investigation as you discuss them—paint tools, shape tools, and so on.

Select Video Workshop Scene Maker
Import **your illustration**
Select a background
Save **your scene**

3 *Now you can put your drawing into a scene.* Discuss the Video Workshop Scene Maker toolbar. Let a few students demonstrate how to add text and choose different fonts, colors, styles, sizes, and backgrounds after they have inserted their illustration.

Click the microphone icon
Select Record
Record your narration
Save **your narration**

4 *What kind of sound would go with your scene? What could you say about it?* Pick a volunteer to narrate the scene.

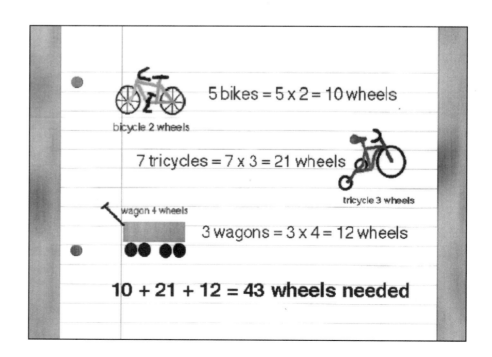

5 bikes = 5 x 2 = 10 wheels

bicycle 2 wheels

7 tricycles = 7 x 3 = 21 wheels

tricycle 3 wheels

wagon 4 wheels

3 wagons = 3 x 4 = 12 wheels

10 + 21 + 12 = 43 wheels needed

Open Libraries
Choose Photographs **or** Clip Art
Import **your photo or art**
Save **your scene**

Select Video Workshop Sequencer
Import **your scene**
Select a transition
Place your transition
Save **your movie**

Click on a place on the soundtrack
Open Libraries
Open Sound
Select some sound or music
Save **your movie**

Open Playback
Click Save & Play
Select Auto Play

THINKING ABOUT THE INVESTIGATION...

5 Tell the students they can create other scenes and import photos into these scenes. ***Can you find a category and photo that is related to bicycles?***

6 ***After you have made several scenes, put them together to make a video presentation. Think about what order you want your scenes to be in. Which one do you think should go first? second?*** Have students place several scenes and transitions in the Sequencer.

7 ***Import your narration. You can even add sound and music to your presentation.***

8 ***When you're finished, we can watch your creation!***

At the end of the investigation, invite pairs to convince the "owner" (played by another student) that their solution makes sense.

- ***Tell about your strategy to solve this problem.***
- ***Did anyone use a different strategy?***

How did you use the computer to convince the owner that your advice will work?

" *We wrote our equations over the scene, showing what we multiplied. Like 7 x 3 = 21 for tricycles.* "

" *Yeah, and then we explained it in more detail, narrating into the microphone.* "

Convince me!

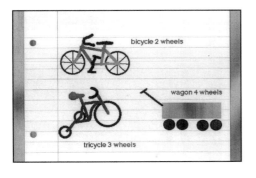

bicycle 2 wheels

wagon 4 wheels

tricycle 3 wheels

to be... ANd, or, Not... to be

USING LOGICAL OPERATORS TO SORT ATTRIBUTE CARDS

WHAT IS THIS INVESTIGATION ABOUT?

This investigation is packed with logical thinking. Crazy Creatures come in 3 species, in 4 colors, and with 1, 2, or 3 legs. How can we figure out all the combinations of those attributes and produce our own complete set of Creature Cards? It's pretty dramatic when the puzzle presentation is animated!

PLANNING FOR THE INVESTIGATION...

Paper	full sheets of paper, colored paper
Supplies	36 unlined note cards (3" x 5") for each pair
Software	*The Multimedia Workshop*
Preparation	Cut several sheets of same-colored paper into 3 strips. Label one strip **and,** one **or,** and the last one **not.** Cut several full sheets of paper in half lengthwise to be used as attribute label cards. Write How to Make Logic Puzzles (page 43) on chart paper.

before the investigation...

The creatures on the planet Boole are strange-looking things. There are three different species: Googlies, Squiggles, and Tri-guys. Draw the three body types and label each with its species name. The creatures can be either blue, yellow, green, or red and have either 1, 2, or 3 legs. What do all the different creatures on Boole look like? Have the students draw as many different Boolean creatures as they can imagine. Ask students to describe their creatures by species, color, and number of legs. Draw the creatures they describe on an overhead transparency. Continue till you have drawn a complete set on the transparency.

INITIATING THE INVESTIGATION...

We make our own *complete* set of Creature Cards by keeping track of attributes. After we learn about operators, we are ready to make sorting puzzles at the computer.

Googly, Squiggle, Tri-guy

red, blue, green, yellow

1 leg, 2 legs, 3 legs

1 ***The set of creatures I have drawn on the overhead projector is called an attribute set. That means that we have all the different combinations we can make with a certain set of characteristics.*** Have the students work in pairs to make their own set of Creature Cards. On the chalkboard, write these attributes: Googly, Squiggle, Tri-guy; red, blue, green, yellow; and 1 leg, 2 legs, 3 legs. As the students work, ask the pairs about the attributes of the Creatures they are drawing.

▶ You may need to help the students find useful ways of reading categories that include the operator cards. Emphasize the fact that **either** goes with **or**, and **both** goes with **and. 2 legs and Googly** may be read as "A creature who has *both* two legs *and* is Googly."

2 ***Now we'll sort our Creatures.*** Make label cards for these attributes: species, color, number of legs. ***We'll call these cards the "attribute labels."*** Show the students the colored *and, or,* and *not* strips you have prepared. ***These cards are called the "operators." Let's use the operators along with the label cards to set up some sorting categories for our creatures.*** Tape the label cards and the operator cards to the chalkboard to identify some sorting categories. Have students sort their cards. Change the sorting categories several times until the students seem fairly confident with the operators.

3 ***Make attribute label cards and operator cards to go with your Creature Cards. What attribute labels could you use with your creatures?*** (Squiggle, blue, 3 legs) ***What would the operator cards say?*** (*and, or,* and *not*)

4 Once students have made their label and operator cards, give an example of a logic puzzle using the guidelines you've written on the chart paper. Let the class as a group help you solve some puzzles. Have pairs work together with their set of creature cards and label and operator cards to make up their own sorting puzzles.

INTEGRATING SOFTWARE INTO THE INVESTIGATION...

We make Creature puzzles on the computer. Animated puzzles with dramatic transitions make for exciting solutions!

Open ***The Multimedia Workshop***
Select Paint Workshop
Create your illustration
Save **your illustration**

1 *Now let's make Creature Card sorting puzzles for each other on the computer. Let's think about how we could use the computer to make our creatures.* Students can make illustrations that mimic their Creature Cards. The software tools make it easy to modify the Creatures by color and number of legs. Students can type the attributes on the illustrations if they want, to remind their audience (or themselves!) of how they are sorting.

Select Video Workshop Scene
   Maker
Import **your illustration**
Select a background
Type in your text
Save **your scene**

2 To make a movie, the students must put their illustrations into scenes. **Add backgrounds to the scenes and be sure to save each one with its own name.** Students may want to add a title scene and scenes that give written clues. Remind them to provide the answer to their puzzle as the last scene.

Select Video Workshop Sequencer
Click on the first box on the
   video track
Import **your scene**
Select a transition
Place your transition
Save **your movie**

3 *After you have made several scenes, move to the Video Workshop Sequencer and put all your scenes together to make a movie.* Have students place several scenes and transitions in the Sequencer. Adding sound is fun, especially if a microphone is available and students can narrate their own work.

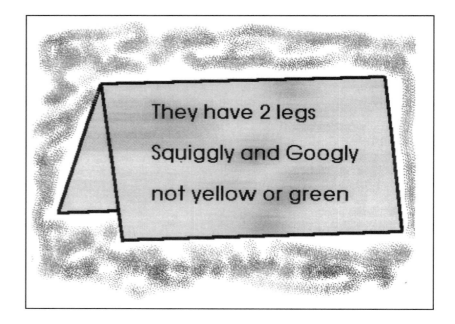

They have 2 legs

Squiggly and Googly

not yellow or green

Now let's watch our presentations and see if we can guess the attributes and operators in the puzzles. Just before the last scene, stop the action by pressing the control key and typing a period. Let the students try to come up with some solutions to the puzzle and then run the finale.

THINKING ABOUT THE INVESTIGATION...

Toward the end of the investigation, review the presentations. Talk with the students about their work and what they learned.

- *How did you keep track of which cards you needed to make to have a complete set?*
- *What did you find out about sorting by using the operator cards?*

What part of the computer presentation was the most fun?

 " Making the drawings of the Creatures. And pouring in the different colors. "

 " Putting the sound to match the clues. "

How about the rest of you?

Did you figur it out?

Red Squiggly, Blue Squiggly, Blue Googly, Red Googly and all of them have 2 legs.

thousands collections

COLLECTING AND DISPLAYING ONE THOUSAND ITEMS

WHAT IS THIS INVESTIGATION ABOUT?

What does one thousand of something look like? We collect 1000 items and find that the way they look can differ greatly, depending on what the 1000 items are! We find creative ways to count efficiently, keep track of what we have already counted, and display our Thousands Collections so that we can see, without having to count each item, that there are 1000. Our computer presentations add a lot to our understanding of big numbers.

PLANNING FOR THE INVESTIGATION...

Paper	full sheets of paper, chart paper
Software	*The Multimedia Workshop*
Preparation	Have general supplies available that the students might need for counting and for creating their displays, such as tape, cups, or large pieces of butcher paper.

before the investigation...

Have a brainstorming session on ideas for Thousands Collections. As the students suggest items to collect and organize, record their ideas on chart paper.

Ideas for Thousands Collections

draw stars

beans

buttons

spiders

baseball cards

LinkerCube rows

INITIATING THE INVESTIGATION...

We make collections of 1000 items. It seems like an impossibly huge task till we have a plan. Then the challenge is how to keep track of it all!

> **Some groups may choose a collection that you doubt they will be able to complete. Don't worry or intervene with their plans. Let them know that revising their plan is part of understanding what 1000 really is.**

1 *Each group of four will collect or make 1000 things and then make a display that proves you have 1000. Let's look at our list of suggestions for our Thousand Collections.* Have the groups choose an idea from the list or another idea they agree on.

2 *What are some ways you might show your collection?* Tell them to make a plan that tells how they will collect and display the 1000 things. *Have someone in your group write about how you will collect and display your items. Also make a list of materials you will need to make your display, such as tape, cups, or large pieces of butcher paper.*

> **Encourage the students to use various counting strategies. Some will adopt counting strategies that involve groups, such as putting items into groups of ten and then counting by tens. As these strategies are shared, other students will have the opportunity to consider them.**

3 Give the group some time to collect, count, and record their collections. As they work, visit with the groups individually and discuss what they're doing. *How many items do you have for your collection so far? How are you keeping track of the number of items? How much space do you think your collection will need?* (Imagine a collection of 1000 inflated balloons!)

4 As the students finish their Thousands Collections displays, take a tour of the classroom and discuss the ways different groups solved difficulties that came up as they worked.

This is 100

There are 10 100's in this bag = 1000!

INTEGRATING SOFTWARE INTO THE INVESTIGATION...

We find even more moving ways to show 1000. Some of us are content with picture proof, but others produce a movie—sound and all—to show what they've done.

1. Have the groups brainstorm about ways to show 1000 on the computer. *What computer tools could you use to show so many items? Talk to your group about how you want your pictures or movie to look. Use notes and sketches to remind you of ways to organize your Thousand Collection on the computer.*

Open **The Multimedia Workshop**
Select Paint Workshop
Create your illustration
Save **your illustration**
Open Libraries
Import **clip art**
Save **your illustration**

2. Some students may want to work only in the **Paint Workshop** to create one or several images (either their own creations, clip art, or photographs) to show their Thousands Collections.

Select Video Workshop Scene Maker
Import **your illustration**
Select a background
Type in your text
Save **your scene**
Select Video Workshop Sequencer
Import **your scene**
Select a transition
Place your transition
Save **your movie**

3. Other students may feel comfortable making several scenes in the **Video Workshop Scene Maker** and then using the **Sequencer** to animate their scenes. The most sophisticated users could add transitions and sounds and music for a very elaborate presentation.

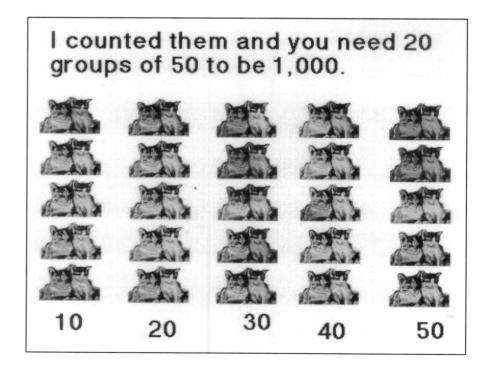

I counted them and you need 20 groups of 50 to be 1,000.

10   20   30   40   50

Select Writing Workshop
Select Print

Open Playback
Click Save & Play
Select Auto Play

THINKING ABOUT THE INVESTIGATION...

4 Students who created only an illustration may want to write about their collection and then print their Thousands Collections illustrations at the end of the investigation.

5 If some students have made movies, choose a time when the entire class can watch their presentations. *Let's watch these movies to see other ways to understand 1000.*

Toward the end of the investigation, review the presentations. Talk with the students about their work and what they learned.

- *What new things did you learn about big numbers?*
- *How can you tell there are 1000 items here without counting them?*

What was the hardest part of the investigation?

 " Keeping track of the buttons. We forgot which ones we counted. Then we put them in cups so we only had to count by hundreds."

 " Remembering how many Cut and Pastes we should do."

 " We made a movie. It went too fast so it was hard to count the thousand."

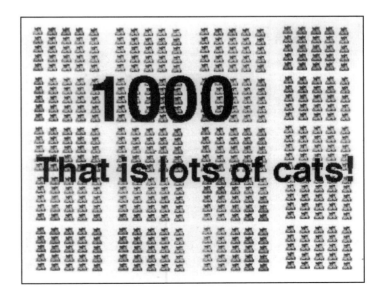

design a dream House

SOLVING AREA PROBLEMS

WHAT IS THIS INVESTIGATION ABOUT?

Approximating is important to us as we design the floor plans for our dream houses. *About* what area should we make the kitchen? If the bathroom is *about* half the area of the bedroom, what will the area be? We use Rainbow Tiles to help us visualize the areas and make our own computations. Later, we organize the areas we have on a spreadsheet and let the computer make the computations!

PLANNING FOR THE INVESTIGATION...

Manipulatives Kit	*For each pair:* 100 Rainbow Tiles in mixed colors
Paper	17" × 22" 1-inch grid paper, 12" × 18" construction paper
Software	*The Cruncher*
Preparation	Make a copy of How to Make Plans for Your Dream House (page 44) for each pair.

before the investigation...

Close your eyes and imagine that your are inside your dream house. **Let's name the rooms.** On the chalkboard, write the name of the rooms as the students say them. **Now open your eyes. Which of these rooms do you think would be the largest? the smallest?** Talk briefly about what a floor plan is. As students discuss the floor plan, encourage them to use the language of area: *dimension, length,* and *width.*

INITIATING THE INVESTIGATION...

We let our imaginations expand as we design a floor plan and then figure out the areas for each of our imaginary rooms.

1 *Pretend you are architects designing your dream house. First you need to design a floor plan. You have 50 Rainbow Tiles to lay out your floor plan. Think about what the area of each room might be as you work.*

2 On the chalkboard, draw several tiles in the shape of a rectangle. Erase the drawing and have the students build the same shape with their tiles. **What's the area of this room?** Repeat the process several times, showing a different shape each time.

3 *When you've completed your floor plan with tiles, make a set of architect's plans for your house using grid paper.* Distribute and go over the directions for How to Make Plans for Your Dream House.

4 When students finish their recordings, have the pairs bring them to the circle to share with the class.

> ▶ Figuring out a way to translate how the tiles look to the grid paper requires students to use good thinking skills. Some students may notice that they can count the number of tiles and then count the number of squares on the grid paper. Others may use length and width as a shortcut. Accept the different levels of approaches, all the while encouraging students to expand their thinking.

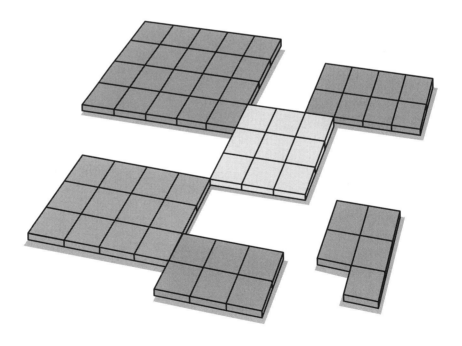

INTEGRATING SOFTWARE INTO THE INVESTIGATION...

We make a spreadsheet and a graph of our dream houses that show us another way to think about area.

Open *The Cruncher*
Select New Spreadsheet

1 *Using your set of plans, I'd like you to organize the information into a spreadsheet and bar graph on the computer.* Discuss with the students the meaning of a *spreadsheet* (a grid made of rows and columns) and *cell* (a small rectangle within the rows and columns). Show them a sample on *The Cruncher.* **We'll do one together and then you can design your own.**

Select a cell
Type your title in the cell
Click on the check
Select Save

2 *What do you think would be a good title to enter into a cell?* Type in a title that students suggest.

Select a cell
Type your heading in the cell
Click on the check
Select Save

3 *What column heading could we enter for the rooms? Then let's list all the rooms in the house.* Enter the column heading in the first column and demonstrate to the students how to enter a few rooms—my bedroom, living room, kitchen, and so on.

Select a cell
Type your data in the cell
Click on the check
Select Save

4 *Decide how you want to record the areas you have. How did you figure the area?* If students multiplied to get the area, they could title the column Length times Width. Tell them that on the computer, an asterisk is the symbol that stands for "times" and that they should type in this symbol between the numbers for length and width (for example, 3*4). If students counted, they could enter the number under a column with the heading Number of Squares. **Enter the actual data in the labeled columns for each room.** Let volunteers enter the data for several rooms.

	A	B	C	D	E	F
1			My Dream Home			
2						
3	Room	length	width	area		
4						
5	living room	3	3	9		
6	kitchen	2	2	4		
7	bathroom	2	2	4		
8	my room	2	2	4		
9	moms room	3	2	6		
10	sisters room	2	2	4		
11	brothers roo	2	2	4		
12	hall	7	1	7		
13	dining room	3	2	6		
14						
15			Total	48		

5 ***How could we get the computer to compute the area of each room for us?*** Demonstrate to students that if they add an equal sign before their data (=3 * 4 or =3 + 3 + 3 + 3) and click the check, the computer will calculate the area for them. Go back and forth between the data and the solutions until students are comfortable with this.

Click Notes
Type in your notes
Select Option
Select Sticker Picker
Choose a sticker
Click OK
Move your sticker

Select File
Select Print

6 ***What could you write in the Notes that would tell about area and your dream house?*** Ask a volunteer to type a short note. ***Use the stickers to decorate your spreadsheet and Notes.*** Demonstrate how to select a sticker and move it around.

7 Have pairs work at the computer to make a spreadsheet like the one the class did together. ***Print your spreadsheet and notes. Add color to them if you'd like. For an extra challenge, try adding the areas of all the rooms together to get the total area of your dream house.***

THINKING ABOUT THE INVESTIGATION...

Toward the end of the investigation, have the students bring their dream house plans and computer printouts to share with the class.

- ***What is the largest room in your dream house? the smallest?***
- ***How did you figure out the total area on your floor plan? How about on the computer?***

How did your computations compare to the computer's?

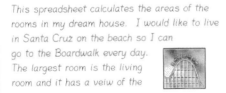

My Dream Home

This spreadsheet calculates the areas of the rooms in my dream house. I would like to live in Santa Cruz on the beach so I can go to the Boardwalk every day. The largest room is the living room and it has a veiw of the ocean.

My room has a door to the beach.

" I added up the area of all the rooms to get the total area. I got a different number on the computer. I found out it was because the area of one of the rooms was not the same as on my plans. "

Quilt Squares

EXPLORING GEOMETRY THROUGH QUILT MAKING

WHAT IS THIS INVESTIGATION ABOUT?

We use simple squares to learn about many aspects of geometry. We get involved with the ideas of tessellation and rotation, and it's even more intriguing to explore these ideas on the computer.

PLANNING FOR THE INVESTIGATION...

Paper
white construction paper cut into 5" × 5" squares, 12" × 18" drawing paper, Quilt Squares grid paper (page 46), full sheets of paper

Supplies
scissors, glue, tape

Software
The Multimedia Workshop

Preparation
Cut many 5" × 5" squares of colored construction paper into triangular eighths. Copy the list of Quilt Explorations (page 45) onto the chalkboard.

before the investigation...

Show the class two colors of the triangles you have prepared and one piece of 5" × 5" white background paper. **Can you make one of these squares out of two colors of triangles? Use equal numbers of each color.** Let pairs experiment, gluing paper triangles onto white background squares to record the different ways they found. Then gather the class together. **How would you describe your design? What does it remind you of?**

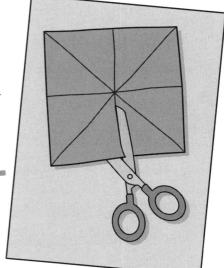

INITIATING THE INVESTIGATION...

We design quilt squares out of small triangles—everyone starts out with the same pieces but we make the final results very different by rotating and tessellating!

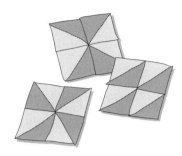

> The concepts of *rotation* (turning as if on an axis), *reflection* (a mirror image), and *tessellation* (mosaic pattern or checkerboard appearance) may arise during this investigation. Many students will be interested in learning the formal math language that goes with the ideas they've brought up. And familiarity with these terms will be helpful when they begin their work at the computer.

1 Have the class take charge of sorting the squares they made before the investigation so that the same designs are together. Choose one group of at least four identical quilt squares. **Let's try to put these squares together to form a quilt. Who has a way of arranging the squares so that they make an interesting pattern?** Ask the students to describe the pattern and tell about the orientation of the squares.

2 **Now it's time to explore this quilting idea a little more. Here are some possibilities.** Go through the Quilt Explorations that you have written on the chalkboard.

3 Have students work together in pairs to do any of the explorations that interest them. **Make sure you complete one exploration idea before you move on to another one.**

4 When they've finished, organize a tour of the class's quilt creations. Give the students ample time to browse among the quilts, enjoying and admiring each other's work.

INTEGRATING SOFTWARE INTO THE INVESTIGATION...

We can make one design on the computer and transform it with just a few clicks. If we want, we can get pretty fancy with pictures, words, sound, and even action.

Open **The Multimedia Workshop**
Select Paint Workshop
Create your illustration
Save **your illustration**

Select Writing Workshop
Choose No Template
Type your story
Import **your illustration**
Save **your story**

> **Some students may want to use only the Paint Workshop, exploring these options and features in depth. Others may want to put their drawings into a presentation. Let the students decide which works best for them.**

1   Have individual students explore a new quilt idea at the computer. Remind students of the useful tools in the **Paint Workshop**: Flip Horizontal, Flip Vertical, Rotate 90°, and Rotate by Degrees. ***Try exploring some of these tools as you make your quilt squares.***

2   Some students may prefer to write a Discovery Summary about their findings. ***Include what you have found out about geometry and quilting.*** They can import a drawing or just write about what they found out as they explored.

3   After the students have been working for a while, bring the class together so the students can update each other on their findings or the computer process. If pairs have found features in the software useful, they may want to share their findings with the class.

Here is my quilt square pattern like a pinwheel

4 Students who used only the **Paint Workshop** may enjoy printing and coloring their quilt squares. For those students who have made a movie, choose a time when the class can watch their presentations.

THINKING ABOUT THE INVESTIGATION...

Toward the end of the investigation, ask the students to tell about their work on the quilt squares.

- *Did your quilt square remind you of anything else you've seen?*
- *Was it harder to make quilts using the cut paper or the computer?*

Tell us about the line of symmetry on your quilt square.

" *This has two lines of symmetry. One is up and down and one is across.* **"**

I can't see them. Can you show me in a different way?

" *I'll divide it into halves with my hand. Does that help?* **"**

Here is my quilt

I used the lasso and copy and flip vertical and flip horizontal and paste

Animal park

DESIGNING MAPS TO SCALE

WHAT IS THIS INVESTIGATION ABOUT?

We plan an Animal Park of our own…to scale! How much space should we set aside for the animal areas? How about space for park visitors? Total space for the park? The grand finale comes when we create a movie to entice visitors to our Animal Park.

PLANNING FOR THE INVESTIGATION…

Manipulatives Kit	*For each group of four:* 90 Rainbow Tiles
Paper	full sheets of paper
Supplies	calculators, 12-inch rulers, masking tape
Software	*The Multimedia Workshop*
Preparation	On chart paper, write the Animal Park Maps information (page 47) and display it. Cut one piece of butcher paper for each group of four students and tape it onto the top of their tables.

before the investigation…

Let's try to construct a map of the classroom using the scale 1 inch = 1 foot. Give students the classroom dimensions, and have them talk you through making an outline of the room on the chalkboard. Choose a desk or cabinet from the room. Show the students how to measure it (rounding off to the nearest foot). Outline it and cut it out. Tape the scaled item in the appropriate place within the classroom outline on the chalkboard.

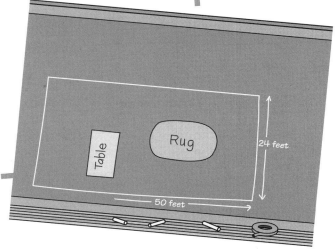

INITIATING THE INVESTIGATION...

We are the designers of an Animal Park. We draw a plan to scale and encounter math at every turn.

> Tell the students that it's acceptable for each group to approach this investigation differently. Keep in mind that a certain amount of struggle is desirable and will promote cooperative thinking.

1. ***Let's design a park for animals and people.*** Discuss the Animal Park Maps specifications you have written on the chart paper so that the students have a clear understanding of the task. Have groups of four students work together. ***Jot down notes, calculations, sketches, and diagrams to keep track of your progress. These will be your Animal Park log notes.***

2. Let students spend time researching and gathering information about animals they want to include in their animal park. Have them include the number data—weight, length, height, number of babies, group size and so on—in their logs.

3. ***Now that you know something about animals, you're ready to tackle your own Animal Park maps. Use Rainbow Tiles to make areas for the animals you want to have in your park.***

4. ***Trace around the outside of the tiles and record the area.*** Have students cut the different areas out of paper, and glue them onto a large piece of butcher paper to make their maps.

5. Toward the end of the investigation, have groups show their maps and logs. Let the class discuss their thinking about how the area in the Animal Park was distributed and how their research on animals helped them make their drawings.

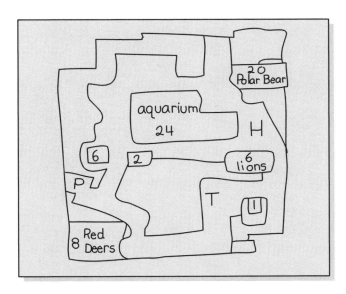

INTEGRATING SOFTWARE INTO THE INVESTIGATION...

Although our paper maps of the Animal Park were interesting, when we add animated photographs and sound, we create a *wild* Animal Park presentation!

Open *The Multimedia Workshop*
Select Paint Workshop
Create your illustration
Open Libraries
Choose clip art or photographs
Save **your illustration**

Select Video Workshop Scene
  Maker
Import **your illustration**
Select a background
Type in your text
Save **your scene**

Click the microphone icon
Select Record
Record your narration
Save **your narration**

Select Video Workshop Scene
  Maker
**Click on the first box on the
  video track**
Import **your scenes**
Select a transition
Place your transition
Save **your movie**

1 ***Using your Animal Park maps, I'd like you to make a movie to draw visitors to your park. Let's start with an animal picture.*** In the Photo Library, the students can find and import animal photographs for their illustration. Other students may prefer to draw their own animals.

2 ***Let's make a scene—all videos are just a series of scenes.*** Discuss the Video Workshop Scene Maker toolbar. Let a few students demonstrate the tools. ***Make several scenes to include in your presentation. You can even add animation to your movie. Look in the Libraries to find Quick Time.***

3 ***Think about what kind of sound you want to go with your scene. What could you say about your scene?*** If a microphone is available, pick a volunteer to narrate a scene.

4 ***Move to the Video Workshop Sequencer and put all your scenes together to make a video presentation.*** Have a student demonstrate placing scenes into the Sequencer. ***Using a transition after the scene allows a smooth transition between scenes.*** Have students place several scenes and transitions in the Sequencer.

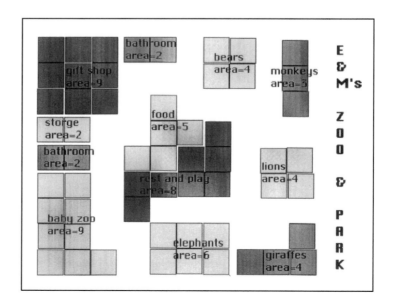

Click on the Soundtrack
Open Libraries
Open Sound
Select a sound or music
Save **your movie**

Open Playback
Select Autoplay

5 *Would you like to add sound and music to the presentation?* If necessary, show students how to place the sound track under the scenes. They can import their narration or select files from the Sounds Library.

6 When all groups have finished their projects, let each one play their video presentations for the class. **Now we are ready to watch our creations!**

THINKING ABOUT THE INVESTIGATION...

Gather the class after the presentations and discuss their thinking with them.

- *What was the hardest part of this investigation? the most fun?*
- *Did you think it was a good rule to allow one-third of the Park for where the animals live? Why or why not?*

Do you think your presentation convinced visitors to come to your Park?

" *Yes, because a movie is more fun to watch than looking at a paper.* "

" *The map was harder to understand on the movie. It was hard to make measurements on it.* "

What part of the presentations did you like best?

tally Ho!

INVESTIGATING PROBABILITY WITH DICE

WHAT IS THIS INVESTIGATION ABOUT?

We roll the dice and learn about an important probability concept—determining possible outcomes. We make predictions, record results, and use the computer to organize and graph our outcomes. By listing the possibilities and maybe even their potential for occurring, we strengthen our ability to make wise choices.

PLANNING FOR THE INVESTIGATION...

Manipulatives Kit *For each pair:*
Numeral Die

Paper full sheets of paper

Software *The Cruncher*

before the investigation...

Pose the following questions to the class: *If we roll a die 100 times, what is likely to happen? Which numbers do you think will come up most often?* Informally discuss ideas about probability with the students. Then list on the chalkboard all of the numbers that may be rolled. Explain that this list is called the *sample space* or possible outcomes. Ask the class to make predictions about which numbers will come up most often and to explain their thinking. Write their predictions on the chalkboard.

INITIATING THE INVESTIGATION...

We roll the dice, make predictions, and then make a chart of our results. We find out what's likely and what's impossible!

> To make good predictions and figure out the probability of something occurring, students should first determine the *sample space,* which in this instance is 1, 2, 3, 4, 5, 6. By modeling the mathematical language *(probability, sample space),* the students learn to understand these terms and may begin to incorporate them into their vocabulary.

1 ***Now let's check out our predictions.*** Let partners work together to roll the die a total of 20 times. After each roll, they should record their results on a sheet of paper. As partners finish, have them come up and put their results on the class chart.

2 Discuss the results on the chart with the class and compare their predictions to their results. ***Which numbers were rolled most often? How does that compare with our predictions? Why do you think certain numbers came up more than others?***

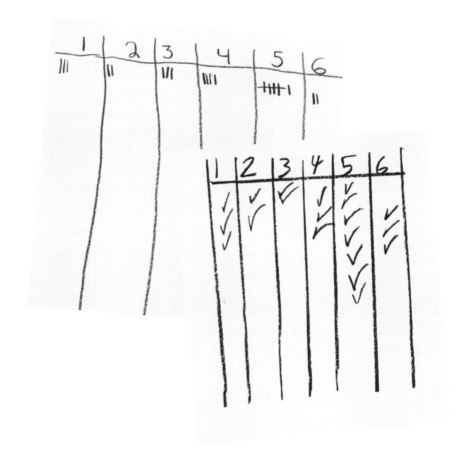

Number Rolled

Group	1	2	3	4	5	6
A	3	2	5	6	3	1
B	1	5	4	3	4	3
C						
D						
E	3	1	3	4	3	6
F	4	5	2	2	1	4

INTEGRATING SOFTWARE INTO THE INVESTIGATION...

We graph our predictions and results on the computer. Our "guessing" gets better and better!

Open *The Cruncher*
Select New Spreadsheet

1 *I'd like you to make a spreadsheet that shows the results on the class chart. Work with your partner to make a sketch of your spreadsheet first.* Remind students of the components of a spreadsheet: rows, columns, and cells. Point out each on *The Cruncher*. *We'll do the results for the numbers 1 and 2 together, and then you can design your own spreadsheet for the numbers 1 through 6.*

Select a cell
Type your title in the cell
Click on the check
Select Save

2 *What do you think would be a good title for the spreadsheet? Let's enter that into a cell.* Type in a title that students suggest.

Select a cell
Type your data in the cell
Click on the check
Select Save

3 *What column heading could we enter? Groups is a good idea for the first one. What about another column heading?* Enter the column heading in the first column and demonstrate to the students how to enter all the groups in the column. Then have a volunteer type in the Number Rolled column. Let volunteers enter the data from the chart into the cells.

Select Options
Select Functions
Choose Sum
Drag the cursor through cells you choose
Click on the check

4 *How could we get the computer to add the numbers for us?* Demonstrate to students how to drag the cursor through the cells in the column. Then choose Sum and specify which cells to add on the formula bar (for example, b4 + b5 + b6 + b7). Go over this process several times, encouraging volunteers to sum up other columns.

	A	B	C	D	E	F	G	H	I	J
1	Results of Dice Rolls									
2	Dice number		1	2	3	4	5	6		
3									Total Roll	
4	Group									
5	power rangers		4	5	0	1	6	4	20	
6	Gladiators		4	4	4	4	4	0	20	
7	charmers		2	1	5	5	5	2	20	
8	Blue Jays		1	2	2	5	6	4	20	
9	Giants		1	2	10	3	3	1	20	
10	A's		4	5	4	3	3	1	20	
11	Total		16	19	25	21	27	12	120	

**Drag the cursor through the
    cells you choose**
Select Options
Select Chart
Click on the type of chart
Type in title
Label the X and Y axis
Click OK

Select Options
Select Sticker Picker
Choose a sticker
Click OK
Move your sticker

Click Notes
Type in your notes
Select Option
Choose a sticker
Click OK
Move your sticker

Select File
Select Print

THINKING ABOUT THE INVESTIGATION...

5 *Let's present our data on a graph.* Show the students how to select the data cells they want to include in the chart (the Total row) by dragging the cursor through them. Have them select the chart type. Let students try several types of graphs and discuss which one makes the most sense. Have them type in a title and X and Y axis labels.

6 *Let's decorate our spreadsheet.* Demonstrate how to select stickers and move them around the spreadsheet to make a pleasing layout.

7 *What could you write in the Notes that would tell about your results when you rolled the die?* Click anywhere in the notebook window and ask a volunteer to type a short note. Show students how to illustrate their notes with stickers.

8 Have students go through this process using some of the other data on the chart. When they complete their spreadsheet, tell them to print their work and color it if they'd like.

Toward the end of the investigation, bring the class together to discuss their spreadsheets and graphs.

- *How did you arrange the data in columns and rows?*
- *How did you get the computer to do the adding?*

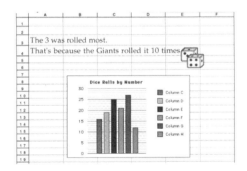

What does your graph show about the number that was rolled the most often? least often?

" *We rolled 6 most often.* **"**

" *Everyone rolled a different number the most often.* **"**

Why do you think that was?

Survey Questions

What sport do you enjoy playing?

What magazine do you like to read?

How many are in your family?

What actor or actress do you like?

What is the best movie you have seen lately?

What is your favorite snack?

What kind of cereal do you like best?

What cartoon character do you like best?

42   SURVEY QUESTIONS ▪ LINKING MATH AND TECHNOLOGY GRADE 3

HOW TO MAKE LOGIC PUZZLES

How to Make Logic Puzzles

1. Fold a sheet of paper in half.

2. Use you label and operator cards to put together a sorting category. Copy the labels onto the front of your puzzle sheet.

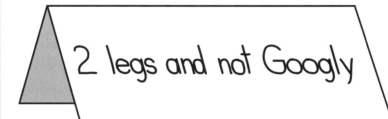

2 legs and not Googly

3. Sort your Creature Cards according to the category you've named.

4. Draw colored sketches of the creatures that fit in the category on the back of your puzzle sheet. (This will be the answer sheet.)

How to Make Plans for Your Dream House

- Cut pieces of grid paper the same size and shape as each room. Write on each piece the name of the room, the dimensions, and the area.

- On construction paper, arrange the grid paper rooms just like the floor plan you designed with tiles. Glue the grid paper onto the construction paper.

- Write a few sentences telling about your dream house. Draw a picture of the outside of your house if you would like.

Quilt Explorations

- Make as many different quilt squares as you can using 2 colors, 4 triangles of each. Find a way to organize your squares into a display.

- Make many quilt squares of the same design. Create a quilt with them.

- Make a "crazy quilt" with squares of different designs.

- Make a quilt square. make lots of small copies of it from quilt squares grid paper. Arrange and rearrange the small quilt squares to see what patterns you could make. Tape together your favorite arrangements.

- Use quilt sqaures grid paper to plan a quilt design. Use your plan to make a regular-sized paper quilt.

- Do you have a quilting idea of your own that you'd like to try? Let me know what it is?

QUILT SQUARES GRID

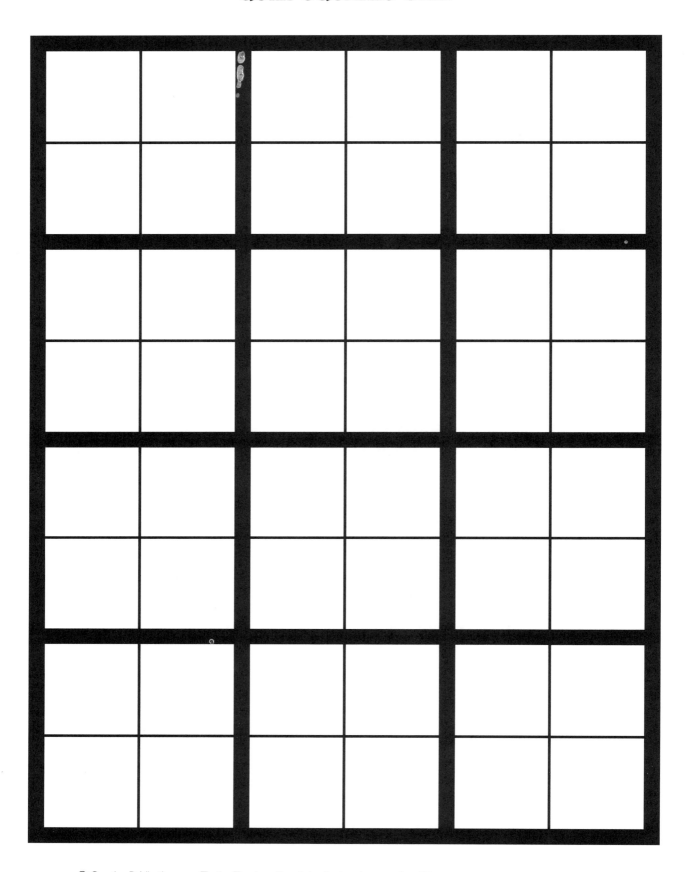

Animal Park Maps

Design a paper map of an Animal Park.

Follow these specifications:

- You may use 90 tiles to outline the shape of your park on your butcher paper. When you have a shape that you like, trace carefully around the outside edges of the tiles to record the shape of your Animal Park, and then push the tiles aside.

- Make enclosures for the animals in your park. They should take up a total of one-third of the park's area.

- The rest of the space will be for the Animal Park visitors to use. You may put in picnic areas, walking paths, rest rooms, play areas, and anything else you like.

What to Find Out

- The total area of your Animal Park
- The total area used for animals
- The total area not used for animals
- Challenge: Pick five areas of your Animal Park. Tell how big each area would be in real life if our scale was 1 inch = 1000 feet.

1-CM GRID

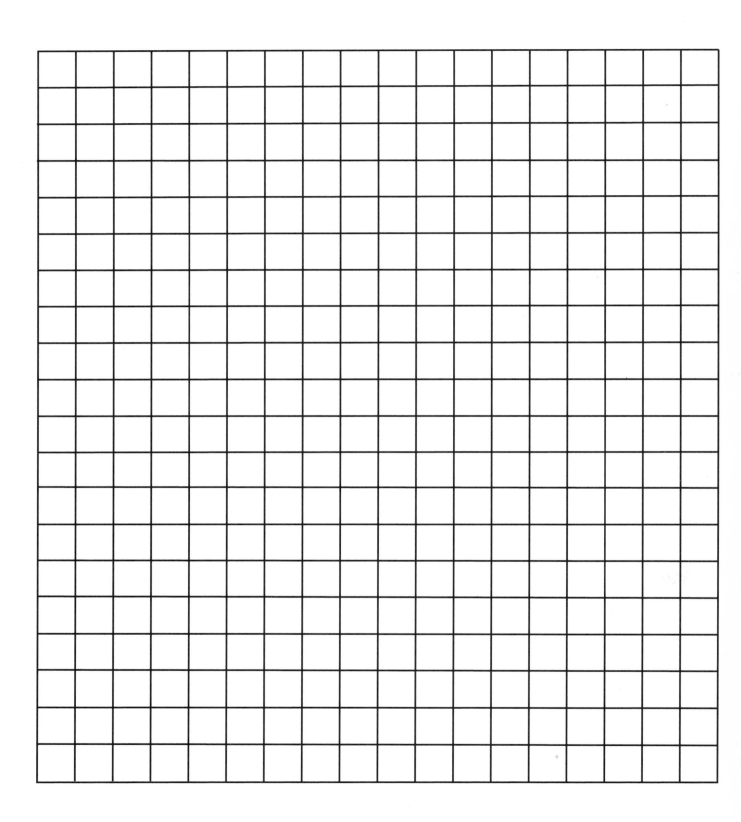

1-CM GRID ▪ LINKING MATH AND TECHNOLOGY GRADE 3